Sing Pop
A Cappella

Book One

Introduction

Some people find it hard to understand how anyone can be a musician without being able to sight-read music. Even so, I know many gifted and talented musicians who cannot read a note. There is no reason for anyone to feel insecure because they cannot read music; sight-reading is undoubtedly a skill useful at all levels of music-making, but not possessing that skill should never exclude anyone from the music-making experience. In an age when digital recorders are often available on phones, PDAs and iPods, there are always other ways of setting down music. Some people even devise their own notation system.

When it comes to transmitting music to other people who may not sight-read well or at all, the traditional practice of 'note bashing' on a piano is something with which many will be familiar. It does the job but arguably it emphasises the 'note value' of the music at the expense of conveying any feeling for, or understanding of the piece; usually these issues are intended to be addressed later.

Personally I found it a revelation when people began to teach me songs not by bashing piano notes, but by singing a line to me and getting me to sing it back several times: no notation but lots of repetition. This method makes teaching songs an option for anyone who can sing and communicate well. That in turn means many singers who do not possess the traditional qualifications of accompaniment and sight-reading skills can still take on the role of choral director. They do not even need a great voice, just an ability to sing in tune and convey the feel of the music.

As I am teaching a song, I indicate the pitch and rhythm with gestures, so adding visual information to the sound. This approach lends itself particularly well to the kinaesthetic learner who usually responds positively to being involved in some form of physical activity and is happy to join in all aspects of this 'call-and-response' process. By contrast those who struggle most with learning songs by ear are those who have been exposed to sight-reading much too early and have consequently almost lost their auditory skills. Fortunately they too can re-learn and in my experience they often discover that it is very satisfying to be reconnected with learning by ear.

One consequence of the growth of teaching/learning by ear has been a rise in popularity of the youth choir and a cappella communities. With many singers feeling more confident about attempting to teach and lead others, the only caveat is that they must be prepared to learn all of the parts of each song themselves before attempting to teach them. One compromise is to appoint a leader per part, which can lighten the load for less experienced leaders.

Almost all my groups work on the 'Comprehensive School' ideal that by mixing very experienced singers with beginners, everyone benefits and we create a true community of singers. There is no audition policy and no requirement to be able to read music. People who have not sung for decades are sandwiched between self-assured and practised singers, and within a matter of weeks their singing and confidence improves beyond measure.

Organising singing sessions requires little in the way of premises and equipment. I like to have enough chairs for the entire group and a wall where I can Blu-Tack sheets of paper or project images from my laptop so everyone can see the words without clutching sheets. The first time I teach an arrangement, I have some form of notation with me, but in general I prefer to memorise it and teach without it as I tend to use my arms and whole body to indicate pitch rhythm and intonation.

Novello Publishing Limited
part of The Music Sales Group
London / New York / Paris / Sydney / Copenhagen / Berlin / Madrid / Hong Kong / Tokyo

A Little Bit on Voice Care

This is not a voice care book, however teaching a cappella can be much harder on the voice. If you are teaching alone you will be using a large range. Remember, you do not always have to sing loud since even in a big space people tend to listen carefully to quiet singing. This means you can use different qualities in your voice as you alternate between loud and soft singing.

Both male and female teachers will face some difficulties singing parts out of their natural range. I will sing bass an octave higher which to me feels as if I am singing in the same place as a bass. For a man teaching all sections of a choir I would suggest that when singing soprano and alto he sings an octave lower if it feels comfortable to do so—falsetto can be hard on the voice if you are singing for any length of time.

The Songs

This book covers some of my popular a cappella arrangements. They have all been tried and tested by singing groups of various ages and numbers. I believe that anyone who is confident that they can sing in time and in tune—and feels enthusiastic about teaching a group—should go for it. The songs range from simple to fairly challenging and I have included notes on experiences I have had when teaching them in the hope that these might prove useful to others.

I certainly don't want to discourage more traditional choirs from dipping into this book. Many of these songs and arrangements can offer a lovely contrast within a programme of classical/traditional pieces. I also believe it is desirable for a choir that spends a lot of time learning from notation to take a break and learn something by ear.

Each song in the book is covered by five tracks on the CD. The first is a full performance; and the remaining four tracks each focus on one of the vocal parts (soprano, alto, tenor, bass). In these performances, the relevant part will feature more prominently, allowing the singer to learn their part more effectively. Experience shows that the practice CDs are very popular. Many choir members like to play them in the car or on iPods when commuting. They enjoy learning their parts by being immersed in the music.

Chasing Cars
Snow Patrol

This is a song for the tenors to shine. With this arrangement, it's more to do with the spaces than the notes. It would have been so easy to clutter it up but it's such a beautiful song that the simplicity of the arrangement should help the essence of the song come through, something that is not always easy to achieve. At the end there are a couple of optional extra parts in the soprano and bass. The choruses are almost hymnal (all the parts singing at the same time) with clear silences between each line. The backings in the verses should be sung softly but still with attack.

Help!
John Lennon and Paul McCartney

This song includes a couple of reassuring unison sections. Never underestimate the power of a bit of unison singing and if an arrangement ever gets too much, singing a section in unison can calm and unify everyone. This arrangement started life off with funny little reggae stabs in the harmonies and all sorts of frippery, but a group I was teaching were struggling, so I just took out the frills. I think it is important to be aware that an arrangement can be changed to suit the group with which you are working. If tenor and bass are proving too many parts, get everyone to sing the bass. The alto part to this song closely resembles the original although many people never really notice it. Learning to listen to music vertically (that is to say distinguishing all the elements that are happening simultaneously) is not always as easy as listening to it horizontally (following the music sequentially). However, a cappella singing like this does give people the opportunity to explore the music both ways.

I Say A Little Prayer
Burt Bacharach and Hal David

This is definitely a song for learning over a couple of sessions or more, but the hard work is definitely worth it. The tune in the verse is shared between the soprano and alto. The other parts have the same rhythm as each other, and together sing a 'backing part'. In the chorus, the soprano and bass share the melody's rhythm while the alto and tenor share the 'backing singer' rhythm. In the middle section ('my darling believe me') the tenor and bass share rhythmic patterns so should be taught one after the other.

The alto shares the tenor and basses pattern for the first half and then joins the sopranos' pattern half way. The end section, I indicate with fingers that the line 'answer my prayer' happens three times before the final 'I'm in love with you' which I indicate with a hand to my heart.

Nobody's Fault But Mine
Traditional

The first and second verses of *Nobody's Fault But Mine* are the same–melody in the soprano, all other parts with backing in harmony. Verse 3 works well with humming and an echo between the sopranos and altos. One little thing to watch out for in the bass part is when the phrase 'If I die and my soul be lost' is repeated for the third time: it is different from the first two times. This needs to be learned really well before you teach it.

Somethin' Stupid
C. Carson Parks

There's a challenge for the basses here, as all they have are the 'dum dums' and wordless parts can be harder to memorise. The tune is in the soprano part except from the second line of the middle section where it jumps to the alto (don't be caught out!). The top three parts all sing the same rhythm. When I teach it I might start with the alto and tenor parts and then add the tune. Sing the tune and alto, then tune and tenor, and then put them together with the bass. I recommend that you do the verse one week and learn the middle section the next.

Chasing Cars

Words & Music by Paul Wilson, Gary Lightbody, Jonathan Quinn,
Nathan Connolly & Tom Simpson
Arranged by Gitika Partington

5

Help!

Words & Music by John Lennon & Paul McCartney
Arranged by Gitika Partington

me. And now my life has changed in oh so ma-ny ways,_____ my in-de-pen-dence seems to

me. Now_____ my life has changed, my in-de-pen - dence seems to

me. dm dm dm dm dm dm dm du dm dm dm dm

me. dm dm dm dm dm dm dm dm dm dm dm dm

D   F#m   Bm

van-ish in the haze. But ev-'ry now and then___ I feel so in-sec-ure,_____

van-ish in the haze. But now and then, I know that

van-ish in the haze. dm dm dm dm dm dm dm dm

van-ish in the haze. dm dm dm dm dm dm dm dm

G C D   D   F#m

Help me get — my feet back on the ground, — won't you please, please help — me.

Help me get — my feet back on the ground, — won't you please, please help — me.

Help me get — my feet back on the ground, — won't you please, please help — me.

Help me get — my feet back on the ground, — won't you please, please help — me.

When I — was young-er so — much youn-ger than — to-day, — I ne-ver need-ed an-y-bo — dy's

When I — was young-er so — much youn-ger than — to-day, — I ne-ver need-ed an-y-bo — dy's

When I — was young-er so — much youn-ger than — to-day, — I ne-ver need-ed an-y-bo — dy's

When I — was young-er so — much youn-ger than — to-day, — I ne-ver need-ed an-y-bo — dy's

down,_____ and I do ap-pre-ci-ate you be-ing 'round._____ Help me get_ my feet back on the

down,_____ and I do ap-pre-ci-ate you be-ing 'round._____ Help me get_ my feet back on the

down,_____ and I do ap-pre-ci-ate you be-ing 'round._____ Help me get_ my feet back on the

down,_____ and I do ap-pre-ci-ate you be-ing 'round._____ Help me get_ my feet back on the

ground,_____ won't you please, please_ help_ me, help me, help me,_____ oo._____

ground,_____ won't you please, please_ help_ me, help me, help me,_____ oo.

ground,_____ won't you please, please_ help_ me, help me, help me,_____ oo.

ground,_____ won't you please, please_ help_ me, help me, help me,_____ oo.

I Say A Little Prayer

Words by Hal David
Music by Burt Bacharach
Arranged by Gitika Partington

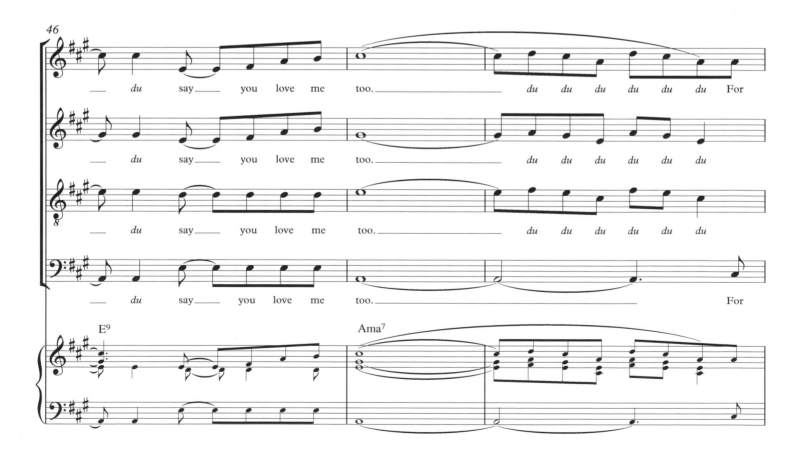

Nobody's Fault But Mine

Traditional
Arranged by Gitika Partington

Somethin' Stupid

Words & Music by C. Carson Parks
Arranged by Gitika Partington

af-ter-wards we drop in-to a qui-et lit-tle place and have a drink or two,_____ and

af-ter-wards we drop in-to a qui-et lit-tle place and have a drink or two,_____ and

af-ter-wards we drop in-to a qui-et lit-tle place and have a drink or two,_____ and

(dm)

A♭   A♭9   A♭7   D♭7   B♭m/A♭   F♭

then I go and spoil it all__ by say-ing some-thing stu-pid like I love_____ you.   I can

then I go and spoil it all__ by say-ing some-thing stu-pid like I love_____ you.   I can

then I go and spoil it all__ by say-ing some-thing stu-pid like I love_____ you.   I can

(dm)

B♭m7   B♭m6   B♭m7   B♭m6   B♭m/A♭   A♭

see it in your eyes that you des-pise the same old lies you heard the night be-fore,___ and

see it in your eyes that you des-pise the same old lies you heard the night be-fore,___ and

see it in your eyes that you des-pise the same old lies you heard the night be-fore,___ and

dm   dm dm   dm dm...

A♭   A♭(add9)   A♭7   D♭7

though it's just a line to you, for me it's true and ne-ver seemed so right be-fore.___ I

though it's just a line to you, for me it's true and ne-ver seemed so right be-fore.___ I

though it's just a line to you, for me it's true and ne-ver seemed so right be-fore.___ I

(dm)

B♭   B7   Fm/E♭   E♭

CD Tracklisting

1-5 **Chasing Cars**
(Lightbody/Connolly/Quinn/Wilson/Simpson)
Universal Music Publishing BL Limited

6-10 **Help!**
(Lennon/McCartney)
Sony/ATV Music Publishing (UK) Limited

11-15 **I Say A Little Prayer**
(David/Bacharach)
Universal/MCA Music Limited/Warner/Chappell Music Publishing Limited

16-20 **Nobody's Fault But Mine**
(Traditional/Partington)
Novello & Company Limited

21-25 **Somethin' Stupid**
(Parks)
Montclare Music Company Limited

Published by
Novello Publishing Limited
14-15 Berners Street,
London W1T 3LJ, UK.

Exclusive Distributors:
Music Sales Limited
Distribution Centre, Newmarket Road,
Bury St Edmunds, Suffolk IP33 3YB, UK.
Music Sales Pty Limited
20 Resolution Drive, Caringbah,
NSW 2229, Australia.

Order No. NOV161513
ISBN 978-1-84938-169-7

Cover Design by Ruth Keating.

Printed in the EU.

Your Guarantee of Quality
As publishers, we strive to produce every book to the
highest commercial standards.
This book has been carefully designed to minimise awkward
page turns and to make playing from it a real pleasure.
Particular care has been given to specifying acid-free, neutral-sized paper
made from pulps which have not been elemental chlorine bleached.
This pulp is from farmed sustainable forests and was
produced with special regard for the environment.
Throughout, the printing and binding have been planned to
ensure a sturdy, attractive publication which should give years of enjoyment.
If your copy fails to meet our high standards,
please inform us and we will gladly replace it.

www.chesternovello.com